LIVING THE
SINGLE LIFE

JULIA MORGAN

Concept development, editing, design and production by CWR

Cover image: CWR

Printed in the UK by Bookmarque

ISBN: 978-1-85345-540-7

CONTENTS

FOREWORD

In 1994, God called me to His ministry vocationally. I knew beyond a shadow of a doubt that God pricked my heart for high school and junior high students. I fully expected that I would be a youth pastor for my entire ministry career. Yet, in the spring of 2001, God rocked my world when he called me out of youth ministry and into singles' ministry. Ministering to single adults was never even on my radar. I always saw singles' ministry as the home of those who 'had something wrong with them'. Little did I know at the time how God would change my life and love for single adults. God, in the following years, gave me a glimpse into what I believe to be His heart and plan for single adults.

For the past eight years, God has allowed me to see the needs of a growing single adult community and how to meet them. This journey ultimately led me to being the single adults' pastor at Saddleback Church in Lake Forest, California. Saddleback arguably has the largest concentration of single adults of any church in the USA. Over 16,000 single adults attend the church, and of those, over 5,000 are involved in small groups (whether singles only or mixed with married couples) on a consistent basis.

As I began singles' ministry, I quickly realized there was not much out there that spoke directly to the needs of single adults. That is until now. Julia Morgan, in her book *One – Living the Single Life*, hits the nail on the head. It is evident to me that Julia has received the same glimpse of God's heart and plan for single adults as I did. The words that you will read on the following pages are words of truth, encouragement, honesty and hope. Her perspective is that of a single adult and the testimonies are authentic to the core.

If you search the word 'single', on any of the major search engines on line, you will find thousands of entries dealing with dating. Julia communicates so eloquently in her book that living the single life is so much more than dating. The season of singleness can be one of the most full and fulfilling times of one's life. God's plan for every adult living in this season of singleness is to realize his or her potential to impact the world with the cause of Jesus Christ like none other. I believe this to the very core of my being. I firmly believe that this work has been crafted by God in Julia's heart. You will be both blessed and encouraged as you read this book.

Clayton Coates
Former singles' and Post-College Pastor,
Saddleback Church, California

INTRODUCTION

SOME YEARS AGO, a Christian friend who had been praying for me described an impression that she felt God had given to her. She saw me sitting by a stream; something shiny had caught my eye. I had dug it out and found that underneath the layers of mud and moss was a precious jewel. I had tried to wash it in the bubbling stream but it had remained filthy dirty. Then I had begun to weep over it and, slowly, it had become clean. My life tears, she said, would polish the jewel as no other cleansing fluid could. My friend said she believed that this was a goal; the jewel was a precious gift and the picture was about how I might realise its value.

Shortly afterwards, another Christian shared with me an impression that he had had of a person with a stone in their hand; the stone appeared to be worthless. However, as their hand opened up, light shone from what was actually a precious jewel.

In the same week, an ornament in someone's home captured my attention. It was an open oyster shell with a pearl, a precious stone, inside.

Sensing that God was speaking to me through these three incidents, I spent time praying about them. Very soon the thought came to me that God wanted to change my view of singleness. Maybe the precious stone stood for singleness but in my mind, and in the minds of many other people, it was often covered in 'mud' through prejudice and wrong perceptions.

I was in my thirties at the time, and was struggling with not being married. From childhood, I had had my life mapped out. I would teach young children until I was twenty-six, then I would be swept off my feet by a tall, dark, handsome stranger. We would be married and have two children, a boy named Simon and a girl named Rebecca, and we would live happily ever after!

A decade had passed and still my dreams had not materialised. I was very fulfilled in teaching, was enjoying life in general, and yet something was missing – I wanted to be married. Like many single people, I had been invited to countless friends' weddings by this time, but was now wondering if God had forgotten that He had created me! I had begun asking Him some serious questions:

- What about the promise in Psalm 37:4 which states that if you delight yourself in the Lord, He will give you the desires of your heart?
- What about Genesis 2:18, where we read 'It is not good for the man to be alone ...'?
- What about Ecclesiastes 4:9 which states 'Two are better than one'?
- 'Why have you forgotten me?' (See Psalm 42:9.)

I pondered these questions and asked myself some too:

- Do I really delight myself in the Lord?
- If I delight myself in the Lord, will He put His desires in my heart, or will I insist on keeping mine?
- Do I really recognise and acknowledge God's Lordship over my life?
- Does it say anywhere in the Bible that we all have to be married?
- Do the 'two' in Ecclesiastes 4:9 mention husband and wife, or could they be friends?

I then decided to set aside any spare time I had to read and pray around the issue of singleness and marriage. This book outlines my own journey as a single person, but also explores some of the honest struggles and victories of other people, whether they are single as a result of being unmarried, widowed, divorced or separated. Each of us has the God-given gift of one life! Whilst we cannot always control our circumstances, we can make choices regarding our attitudes and actions – whether to serve wholeheartedly the one true God, whatever that may mean for us, and wherever it may take us, or whether to live primarily for ourselves and our own desires.

CHAPTER 1

THE SINGLES SCENE

'Did you know that there is no other group within the local church that is able to do more for God's Kingdom and to fulfil God's purposes in the church than single adults? God desires to use single adults in a big way,' says Clayton Coates, former pastor to 2,000 singles in Saddleback Church in California.[1] It is so refreshing to hear such a positive approach to singleness.

Until recently, societal emphasis on marriage and family has caused single adults to feel ostracised from mainstream society. The expectation has been that everyone is married or about to be wed. Clearly, this is God's best for the majority of people – but not necessarily for all. I know, without any doubt, that marriage is a building block for society and I am 100 per cent in favour of it for most people. It also provides us with a picture of Christ and His Church. We can learn so much about God's character through the institution of marriage.

Single groups in society

Sadly, values in society have changed dramatically in recent years so that marriage is often postponed or even ignored, and cohabitation is acceptable – the divorce rate in the UK is one of the highest in Europe. The number of people in Britain choosing to marry is at an all-time low. Many young people have grown up in families where divorce has brought much pain and anguish, so they are reluctant to commit themselves to a lifelong relationship. Others are pursuing careers, caring for elderly relatives, haven't met the right person yet, or have chosen to remain single. Consequently, there is a high proportion of people who are on their own for various reasons. They are:

- widowed
- divorced
- separated
- called by God to be single
- single due to circumstances
- single due to chronic illness or severe disability
- vocational singles, eg nuns, monks, priests
- awaiting marriage in the near future.

Singleness has now become more a part of the culture with television programmes, books and even packaged foods providing for the needs of single people. Nevertheless, many men and women still struggle to come to terms with the thought, or the reality, of singleness. Until it is viewed as an equally viable lifestyle to marriage, singles will continue to feel marginalised.

Some statistics

- The Office for National Statistics for England and Wales (www.statistics.gov.uk) reports that single households have nearly trebled between 1971 and 2008.
- The number of one-person households has been increasing worldwide. By 2020 the number is forecast to reach 253.8 million (www.euromonitor.com/One_person_households).
- Marriage rates in England and Wales have fallen to the lowest level since records began, according to provisional figures for 2007 (www.statistics.gov.uk).
- The Social Trends Report issued in 2009 stated that 24 per cent of people below the age of thirty were married, whereas in 1971, 75 per cent of women were married by the age of twenty-five.

- The same report stated that the number of married couples is at the lowest level since 1895 with 237,000 marriages in England and Wales in 2006, down from 471,000 during the Second World War.

These trends will have tragic results for our society. It also means that there will be a higher percentage of single people in the Church and in society. It is an area the Church particularly needs to address.

S-i-n gleness

Camerin Courtney quotes on the website **www.christiansinglestoday.com**:

> In a moment of melodrama a couple of years ago, I joked with a single friend that at times voices within Christendom have been so silent or judgmental about singleness, that I suspect that they thought the s-i-n at the beginning of the word was no mistake.[2]

Whilst this book seeks to address the issue of those who have not been married, much of it is relevant for people who find themselves on their own, just one, for whatever reason. Each single person will find themselves in unique circumstances, often one of very few in an age group within their church or neighbourhood. Let us remember that everyone will be single at some point in their life, and for eternity.

All of us are called to be a part of God's family, alongside married couples. God's family is much wider than the nuclear family; it is an extended family of believers. God has a plan and a purpose for every individual. After an initial battle over singleness, Corrie ten Boom said, in her book

Tramp for the Lord: 'the Lord had other plans for me than married life.'[3] Understanding one another's status is vital for harmonious relationships – and to avoid misunderstanding and stereotyping.

Support for singles in the Church

Rarely have I heard a sermon on singleness or an illustration referring to singles in a talk. Excellent marriage courses are available, but very rarely anything to support single people. The majority of church leaders are married so have less understanding of singleness.

If the married status, a precious gift, is presented as the only way to happiness and the single state as second best and problematic, we are not being true to Scripture. Neither, however, should singleness be presented as the privilege of the spiritually elite. Both states are equally good. John Stott, a single man who is a well-known Church leader and writer, claims that Scripture bears this out. I wanted to prove this for myself.

Our perception of singleness

I firmly believe that our perception of singleness will largely determine our ability to function and bring glory to God in His kingdom. If we fall under the oppressive umbrella of negative comments about singleness we will enter a lifelong waiting room, stunted in our thinking, paralysed in our actions and unfulfilled in our emotional and spiritual lives.

However long we are single it can be a special time, whether it is near the beginning, in the middle, or at the end of our life. Joshua Harris, in his book *I Kissed Dating Goodbye*, says,

> God gave us singleness as a season in our lives
> unmatched in its boundless opportunities for growth,
> learning and service but we view it as a chance to get
> bogged down in finding and keeping boyfriends and
> girlfriends.[4]

Perhaps one of the most high-profile Christians today is Sir
Cliff Richard who, in his book *My Life, My Way*, looks back
over many years of being single and says, 'It's the lifestyle
I have chosen and I love it.' He rightly says that marriage
is 'committing yourself to someone for the rest of your
life – giving them the right to know where you're going,
what you're thinking and what you are feeling'.[5] As he has
watched a number of his friends getting divorced, he has
remained convinced that singleness was best for him; he was
often away on tours of several months, a lifestyle which is not
always conducive to a strong marriage.

Anthony's testimony

The true benefits of being single can only be realised
if you don't let singleness define you. It is not a condition
to be cured or a problem to be solved. Just enjoy it.
Being single is a position of great opportunity and I bet
current singles would kick themselves if and when they
get married if they failed to realise its benefits.

I'm sure being married can be great, but the fact
is that being single really isn't that bad! I'm not sure
that any of the things that I have done in my adult life
would have been impossible if I weren't single, but I
am pretty sure being single made it a lot easier. My
university career lasted a grand total of six years and
took in four universities in four different cities (and

two countries) along the way. I can imagine this kind of gallivanting could be the source of some chagrin with the other half. The friends I had whilst I was abroad who had partners back in their home countries had to invest a lot of time and energy (not to mention cash) in keeping their relationships going. Unfortunately, it was also generally with limited success. The upshot of my educational career is a very broad group of friends who are strewn across the world. Keeping up with so many different people is tricky, but it lends itself to a large amount of foreign travel and I can't speak highly enough of that.

Mary's testimony

I left home to be married in my mid-twenties and enjoyed over fifty years of very happy married life, but then my world shattered when my husband died very suddenly, totally unexpectedly. For the first time in my life I was physically alone, bewildered and fearful of the future. Through the numbness of grief, God seemed far away even though I knew His promise never to leave me or forsake me.

A friend gave me a copy of the poem 'Footprints' which describes a man dreaming that he was walking along a beach with the Lord, but in the saddest times there was only one set of footprints. On asking why this was, the Lord replied that it is at these lowest, saddest times that He actually carries us. I found great comfort in this thought. I determined not to isolate myself but to keep praying to God, reading my Bible daily and maintaining friendships with other people, especially those who shared my faith. God has been so faithful, even though at times it has been challenging to adapt to being one again after being a twosome for more than half a century. I know God still has work for me to do, and that He is Lord of my situation and will take care of me.

Let us be open to change our perceptions if necessary, and to hear God's view of our status at this time and His plans for our future. Let us commit ourselves to making the most of the time, whenever that may be, rather than wishing it away. One God and one single life can make a difference and influence many for good.

CHAPTER 2

THE BIBLICAL PERSPECTIVE ON SINGLENESS

We read in Genesis 1:27 that God 'created man ... male and female' in 'his own image'. In verse 31 of the same chapter, God reflected on His whole creation and said that 'it was very good'. The first man, Adam, was in no way incomplete in himself even though he was just one man but, as we read in Genesis 2:18, God said, 'It is not good for the man to be alone. I will make a helper suitable for him.' The Lord made Eve from the rib He had taken out of Adam. In Genesis 2:24 we then read, 'For this reason a man will leave his father and mother and be united to his wife, and they will become one flesh'.

Throughout Old Testament times marriage was the norm. In Jewish society, everyone was to be married; singleness and barrenness were unthinkable. People married to continue the family name because having an heir was of vital importance. Sarah, Abraham's wife, and Hannah (see 1 Sam. 1–2) struggled with barrenness for this very reason.

Men and women had no tension over career or marriage because they grew up to do what their father or mother did. A single person in a Jewish home would live with several other generations, so would continue to be cared for if they found themselves single (ie widowed etc). The whole family was responsible for them, ideally to get them married if possible!

There was no Hebrew word for 'bachelor', such was the rarity of a single man. Men like Daniel and Nehemiah, however, were thought to have been single. Nehemiah may well have been a eunuch, which was the norm for a male servant in the Persian court, yet he was the one who responded to God's call to rebuild the walls of Jerusalem. He would have been excluded from Temple worship which lay at the very heart of Jewish religion. But in Isaiah 56:3b–5 God says, 'And let not any eunuch complain, "I am only a dry tree." To the eunuchs who keep my Sabbaths, who choose what pleases me and hold fast to my covenant – to them I will give within my temple and its walls a memorial and a name better than sons and daughters; I will give them an everlasting name that will not be cut off.' The very thing which the eunuchs were denied in their society, God gave to them.

The well-known passage in Isaiah 54 referring to the barren woman says, '"Sing, O barren woman, you who never bore a child; burst into song, shout for joy, you who were never in labour; because more are the children of the desolate woman than of her who has a husband," says the LORD' (v.1).

One can have a family of many. Again, God seems to give the opposite to what is expected by society.

New Testament times

God, throughout Scripture, speaks of single people with compassion and understanding, not rebuke or disapproval.

In 1 Corinthians 12:13, Paul writes, 'For we were all baptised by one Spirit into one body – whether Jews or Greeks, slave or free – and we were all given the one Spirit to drink.' God's heart is for us to be one big happy family!

Jesus, who broke all Jewish tradition by remaining single, described three groups of unmarried people in Matthew 19:11–12: 'Some are eunuchs because

- they were born that way;
- others were made that way by men;

and others

- have renounced marriage because of the kingdom of heaven.

The one who can accept this should accept it.'

These groups could refer to those with homosexual tendencies or physical defects; those caring for ageing relatives or other preventing circumstances; and those who have accepted singleness for the sake of the kingdom. The latter group are often more available to go to countries unsuitable for a family, to travel, to work anti-social hours, and to fulfil other specific roles in the kingdom – or to be obedient to God not always knowing exactly why they are called to be single. Jesus acknowledges that it is a hard word to accept.

Other New Testament single people

Likewise, Paul, of whose marital status we are unsure, clearly sees that the single state is advantageous in certain circumstances. The well-known passage in 1 Corinthians 7 speaks of him stating that it is 'good' not to marry (see v.26).

Some Bible translations use the word 'gift' relating to marriage and singleness in 1 Corinthians 7:7. I had always been led to believe that being single was less than God's best, and certainly not a state to be embraced as a gift! The same word 'charisma' is used to refer to spiritual gifts, such as speaking in tongues. So Scripture is clear that marriage and singleness are good.

Jane's testimony

I came to know the Lord as a child and I always wanted to be a teacher. Amidst this, I presumed that one day I would marry and have children of my own.

It was during a Sunday morning service, as a nineteen-year-old student, that I found myself in tears, as I was suddenly overwhelmed by a sense of God's love. In the midst of this, I felt the Lord put a question to me – was I willing to remain single? This was an entirely new thought to me, but such was the sense of God's love that I could only reply, 'Yes.' Over the next week this strong sense of God's presence continued and verses of Scripture jumped off the page for me, including Isaiah 54:5: 'For your Maker is your husband'. This and other verses confirmed to me that the Lord was indeed calling me to be single, that His love could be sufficient, and that He would give me 'spiritual children'.

I was beginning to find the prospect of remaining single more difficult as time went on, and was increasingly aware of a strong maternal instinct that made it painful at times to see parents with their young children. I clung on to the promises that God had given me that He could be sufficient, but the deep sense of His love was often not present, and there were times when I told the Lord I couldn't face what He was asking of me.

The following year, I was reading a book about the gifts of the Holy Spirit, when much to my surprise I saw singleness listed as a gift. I found myself laughing, as suddenly it cast a whole new light on the situation! I had seen singleness as something God had taken away from me, when all the time it was a gift He had given me. It felt as if my world had suddenly turned the right way up, and viewing it in that way has been the key to the peace and joy that I have experienced since.

This is not to say that there haven't been difficult times, and times when I have failed to trust the Lord to meet my needs. But through all the ups and downs, I have learnt that God is utterly faithful, that His love is all-sufficient and I can turn to Him as a husband in the most practical of situations. My understanding of the relationship has matured over the years and, despite my failings, I can now, thirty years later, say that my sense of security in God's love and His sufficiency is the fundamental certainty in my life that gives me a deep joy and peace.

Singleness viewed as a gift is very precious. There were single people in New Testament times, all of whom had to face the same issues as we do today. In Acts 21:9, we read of Philip's four unmarried daughters who prophesied. In Acts 8:26–38, Paul writes about Philip baptising the Ethiopian eunuch. Whether or not we struggle in our earthly life, we have much to look forward to in the future.

The future Church of God

John's vision in Revelation 21 speaks of the most glorious wedding day to which we can all look forward:

> I saw the Holy City, the new Jerusalem, coming down out of heaven from God, prepared as a bride beautifully dressed for her husband. ... One of the seven angels ... said to me, 'Come, I will show you the bride, the wife of the Lamb.' And he carried me away in the Spirit to a mountain great and high, and showed me the Holy City, Jerusalem, coming down out of heaven from God. It shone with the glory of God, and its brilliance was like that of a very precious jewel, like jasper, clear as crystal. ... The wall was made of jasper, and the city of pure gold, as pure as glass. The foundations of the city walls were decorated with every kind of precious stone. ... The twelve gates were twelve pearls, each gate made

of a single pearl. The great street of the city was of pure gold, like transparent glass.

(Rev. 21:2,9–11,18–19,21)

The New Jerusalem is the Church of God of which we, as Christians, are a part. We see the Church in this passage as perfect, magnificent and triumphant, prepared as a bride for her husband.

Married or single, there is a great hope and a future for all of us. Some of us may have to wait longer than others for our wedding day, but it will be worth waiting for!

CHAPTER 3

GOD'S WILL AND FREE CHOICE

In the Old and New Testaments we read of single people, including Jesus, whom God used to bless others and to further His kingdom. But to what extent do we have a choice as to whether we marry or not? Of course we all have free will, so if Mr/Miss Right does appear, we can choose to marry or remain single, but if we acknowledge Jesus as Lord, another factor comes into play. Christians often pay lip service to the sovereignty of God. We long to know God's will, we believe He has a plan for our lives, and yet we sometimes lack the faith to really seek God in case He says something we don't want to hear. We fear He may send us as missionaries into some deep, dark jungle, or He may ask us to give up all our hard-earned wealth, or even ask us to be married or single!

We must always remember that God is our loving Father who wants the very best for us. He knew us and had plans for us before we were even born, as we read in Jeremiah 1:5. Nevertheless, we cannot presume upon God; He takes our prayers of surrender and commitment seriously.

We have no rights to marriage, children or singleness as they are gifts to us from our loving heavenly Father. Years ago, children were brought up to see marriage as something they could automatically expect – although in our modern society, it seems that fewer young people expect a lifelong partnership but merely long for immediate happiness, albeit from short-term relationships. However, in the kingdom of God, we actually have *no* rights; Jesus also tells us to deny ourselves, to take up our cross and to follow Him. He says that whoever wants to save his life will lose it, but whoever loses his life for Him will save it (Luke 9:23–24). Whilst God promises to care for us, He does not promise us an easy time; in fact, He tells us to count the cost before following Jesus. He may ask us to remain single or to be married for the sake of the kingdom.

'Your kingdom come, your will be done'

Some of us pray the sentence in the Lord's Prayer, 'your kingdom come, your will be done on earth as it is in heaven' (Matt. 6:10) through gritted teeth, secretly pleading that God will bring along Mr/Miss Right as the longed-for spouse. We picture Jesus in the Garden of Gethsemane, sweating drops of blood and struggling to consent to the outworking of His Father's will. We imagine that being single is a similar struggle!

Actually, the real meaning behind that part of the Lord's Prayer is very different. We are asking the Lord to fulfil His good pleasure by doing His will. He loves us so much that we have nothing to fear or dread; He gives us grace to fulfil His will.

Carol's testimony

Singleness became a big issue! I had always enjoyed the company of both men and women, but suddenly marriage seemed to dominate my life. I went to see some good friends to pray about it and was asked, 'What matters most – your relationship with the Lord, or your desire for a husband?' Put like that, I had no hesitation in choosing the Lord. I have learnt to know that what God had for me then, what He has for me now, and what He has for me in the future, is the best. Over the years, I have come to appreciate my singleness, and now I love it!

Reasons for being single

When we are wholeheartedly seeking first the kingdom of God (Matt. 6:33), our attitude to being single may become clear. We may feel one of the following:

- I am single now, so will live my life for God, but ultimately I feel that I need someone with whom I can share my life.
- I recognise that I am called to work for God in such a way that marriage would be a distraction; I will receive God's help and grace daily to be single for as long as is right for me.
- I feel called to be single for the rest of my life.

Not many people receive the call to singleness at one particular time, but tend to come to terms with it and appreciate it over a period of years. The few people who feel called to be single for life often know that God has set them apart for a special purpose which can be better carried out by a single person than by a married couple. John Stott's testimony is that he worked continuously for the Lord and eventually realised that marriage may not be for him.

Many people who are single have not chosen that status. And some have found it thrust upon them through the death of a spouse, or through divorce or separation. They began as one, became two, then reverted back to being one.

Faith's testimony

I'm a Jane Austen fan, some would say a hopeless romantic, and always have been. I suppose, like a lot of people, I assumed I would get married at some point. But I was in no hurry. During my early adult life, I was surrounded by wonderful girlfriends and thoroughly enjoyed being single and independent through my university years. Living away from home after graduation, I began to realise that life was moving forwards and people of my age were beginning to find that someone special to share life with. I now felt a growing desire to meet my Mr Darcy. When I finally fell in love and got married that was it, I was a one-man woman. Maybe a little naively, I thought that whatever life threw at us we were together and would help each other through.

After seven years of marriage, which included having two children and coping with financial strains, my world fell apart. My husband announced he was leaving and I no longer had my soulmate, my best friend, to turn to. Fortunately, one other crucial change had happened during those seven years – I had met Someone who was to become my new best friend: Jesus. During the following years I got to know Him well, and found out what a great comforter, provider, listener and companion He is. I was blessed; I was surrounded by friends and family, people who loved me and wanted to help. But it is lonely in the world when all around you are couples and families. Even with my own family around me – my parents, my brother and sister with their spouses and children – I could feel all alone. I felt I lived in no-man's land (please excuse the pun!); I did not belong to the 'married with children' camp, but neither did I belong to the 'young, free and single' camp. I was a single parent for a fortnight and then I got a weekend 'off'. I could fill the days – I became good at being busy – but once the shops were shut, the daylight faded away, the children were in bed and the DVD ended, that's when I was struck by how lonely it was, being one again.

I had some tough questions to ask of God, and

have ridden the emotional roller coaster that all who have gone through divorce will understand. I was angry with God at times; I went from blaming Him to blaming myself. I can understand how people in similar situations feel the need for revenge, maybe masked as justice – but I knew for my sanity, and the children's well-being, I had to ask God to help me work at forgiving my ex-husband and the 'other woman', and allow God to heal me one layer at a time; I did not realise how deep the hurt had gone.

Now, seven years on, I am still one (plus two growing children!) and there are still lonely times, but I look back on my journey and know I would not enjoy my family, the fulfilment of my career, or the joy and the peace I have found, without the grace, mercy and love of my heavenly Father. I have held on to this promise of God's from the Bible – Jeremiah 29:11: '"For I know the plans I have for you," declares the LORD, "plans to prosper you and not to harm you, plans to give you hope and a future."' God has shown me that whether I am single or married, He has good plans for me, and He alone can make my life rewarding and fulfilling.

Pressure on singles

Many Christians have struggled to find Christian partners and have refused to compromise on the verse in 2 Corinthians 6:14, which states that we should not be yoked to an unbeliever, because the very foundations of their lives would be so different, and not necessarily conducive to a harmonious relationship. Others have sought to follow God's leading for their lives whether or not this meant marriage or singleness; whilst being single at present, they do not know what lies ahead.

Families, society and the Church often put great pressure on people to find partners, seeing this as the only way to be fulfilled in life. One only has to look around our nation today to realise that this is not always the case. We can so readily gain the whole world but forfeit our soul (Matt. 16:26). Marriage can be one way for most people to find contentment, but it is not true for all.

It takes sacrifice on everyone's part to allow God to have His way in children's lives. I will always be grateful for my parents who released me to make my own choices with no pressure or control, only unconditional love and acceptance.

God's grace

I met a lady in her sixties who was working in the slums of Bombay. She was one of the happiest, most fulfilled women I have ever met. On hearing her story, it bore out what I have just written. When she was young, God had called her as a missionary to India, but she ignored the promptings of God to remain single; instead, she got married in New Zealand and settled down. Her marriage was not a happy one and she always felt dissatisfied and discontented even through she had everything money could buy. Her husband, sadly, was killed in a plane crash, so she brought up her children on her own. When they had grown up, God called her again to work in India, so here she was as a more mature lady, living very simply yet radiating the love of God to so many. How gracious God is to give us second chances!

The passage in 1 Corinthians 7 clearly gives us a choice as to whether we marry. If we cannot control ourselves, Paul exhorts us to marry. We don't sin by marrying or by staying single. So how do we achieve the balance of God's will for each individual, and our free choice?

God's 'Plan A'

I had been going out with a Christian for some months when I was in my late twenties. Realising that the relationship was moving into a more serious stage, I began asking God whether this really was the right person for me to marry. I felt uneasy. As I prayed, I felt that God was saying that I could marry this man and be happy enough, but it would be God's 'Plan B' for me. I was no 'Plan B' person; I wanted God's best – 'Plan A' and nothing less! I therefore finished the relationship and waited for 'Plan A' to unfold in due course.

However, it became increasingly clear that 'Plan A' did not involve marriage, though I did not necessarily feel called to be single as some people do.

As the years have gone by, I realise how well God knows me and, whilst it has not always been easy to be single, most of the time I love it! Knowing that God is sovereign over our lives is a huge blessing. Who better to counsel us in things of the heart than the Lover of our lives, the Creator of our hormones and the One who sees the future?

Finding and fulfilling God's purposes for our lives requires taking responsibility and making decisions:
a) costly decisions
b) unpopular decisions
c) courageous decisions
d) lonely decisions
e) challenging decisions
f) possibly long-lasting decisions

Elizabeth's testimony

God never told me that I would be single; I don't think I would have been able to accept it, particularly in my twenties. Instead, He has given me grace, strength and encouragement at each step of the way. I haven't felt that the option of marriage is a closed door and that has helped me.

With regard to relationships, there have been times of hope and of disappointment, times of confusion and of brokenness, even grief over the lack of a close relationship or the chance to have a family of my own. However, there have also been times of joy and peace.

Within the Church, as the years go by, the opportunities for meeting a potential partner become fewer. I believe that God could bring the right person across my path at any time. I have met some great Christian men over the years, but haven't met the right one for me. I have prayed and discussed the situation with God many times, so He must have other plans!

A couple of times I thought that I had met a potential husband, but their lack of a Christian faith was the stumbling block.

God has taught me so much, through times of despair and loneliness, about pressing into Him even more. I have learnt to enjoy extended family. I have been available to help family and friends in need, as well as being free to take on new projects and challenges within my work and church situations. I can identify with those who are alone and can understand the benefits and struggles of those with a similar lifestyle.

As the years go by and the biological clock is ticking (or has tocked!), I think God's grace for me to be single has increased accordingly, though I still have 'wobbly'

moments. My secret to survival as a single is to stay close to God, enjoy the independence I have, and be generous with my time for God and for others.

I find it helpful to share the highs and lows with other single people, but also to enjoy friendships with married people whose lives, I have discovered, are not a 'bed of roses'. Talking to a married friend recently was a levelling experience for me. During an honest discussion, we realised that both situations have their challenges and joys. That really helped me to be more at peace in my single state.

Nigel's testimony

I had been married for over twenty years when I found myself going through a divorce and being left on my own with five teenage children. This presented me with many challenges. The most immediate and intense one was coping personally with a feeling of bereavement and loneliness, yet without anyone having died. It was a very difficult time emotionally, having lost my primary relationship, having no legitimate way of replacing it, and not knowing what the future held. Would I have to spend the rest of my life on my own? If a wife or husband dies, a Christian can remarry; but as a divorcé, where did that leave me? There followed years of uncertainty.

I also had sole responsibility for five confused and hurt children, who seemed on the surface to carry on much of the time as if nothing had happened, but who were all coping with a distressing situation in different ways. To add to all this, when the legal side of things started to kick in I was also fighting for finances and, potentially, custody of my children (but due to the circumstances of my soon-to-be ex-wife and the children's ages, custody in my case turned out not to be an issue). I had been a church leader until just before the divorce, and the shame I felt was intense; I felt I had failed my children, my church and God.

I had a choice of how to cope; having been a Christian for over thirty years, I knew I needed to press into God in a way I had never done before. This was the most difficult situation I had faced in my life. I had coped with my father dying very unexpectedly over ten years earlier; I had been made redundant when I was the sole breadwinner in a family with five young children. However, this was the most testing time I had faced.

During this period, I found God in a deeper way than I had experienced before. He provided me with people to talk to and share my problems with. God did not take the situation away, but helped me live through it and come out the other side. One of the most important things I was told was that there is life after divorce – at the time, I felt as if my world had ended.

Continuing to attend church was a real battle for me. I was so ashamed at being a Christian and being divorced that it took a huge effort to actually walk into the church building most weeks. No one criticised me for the situation I was in, but I still felt terrible. It has taken years for me to regain much of my self-esteem in Christian circles; but (seven years on) I am still not completely where I know I should be. It has been said that divorce is the one unforgivable sin. Whilst I know that this is not true, there is so much pain, hurt and damage caused by divorce to so many people,

especially those you are closest to and love the most.
I have found it a huge challenge to overcome all this.
One wise pastor told me, 'You can't hurry emotions'
– how true this is. I wanted to sort everything out as
quickly as possible, but I could not. It has taken years to
work through emotions in myself and my children; the
intensity subsides, but the emotions are still there.

Watching the effect of the divorce on my children has
been very painful. They have coped with it in different
ways and at different speeds. They are having to work
though many extra issues, as well as the ones teenagers
and those in their twenties usually go through.

Since the divorce, I have remarried. When the
divorce was finalised and I had come to the place
in myself to know there was no realistic hope of
reconciliation, I went to my church leaders and asked,
'What is my situation, biblically?' I had looked at it
on my own, including reading the Bible from cover
to cover, and had come to the conclusion that I could
argue the case either way. I was too emotionally
involved in the situation; I wanted to follow and
honour God but I could not trust myself to come up
with an answer after considering the consequences for
so many people if I got it wrong.

My church leaders (after considerable deliberation
on my particular situation and producing a paper on
what the Bible says about divorce) came back to me and
encouraged me to remain single if I could, but said that
they would support me if I wanted to remarry.

To those reading this who are in the situation I was
in, I would encourage you to earnestly seek God to see
if you can remain single, rather than rush into another
marriage thinking that will solve all your problems.

It won't. It will help in some areas, but it will also give you more issues to face and work through that you would not have if you remain single.

I am now married to a wonderful woman who has helped me through so much. However, starting a new relationship, taking on four stepchildren, and merging two families is a massive challenge; we totally underestimated the size of the task, and the length of time it would take to achieve. However, all this is another story.

I could not have got through the last years without God. I still have questions and scars, but I know God loves me (enough to send His Son to die for my sins), is there for me and I am His son.

These testimonies reflect the honest challenges and triumphs of people who have come to accept their single state, or have found a marriage partner. By allowing God into their lives in increasing measure, His faithfulness to them has become apparent, single or married.

God does give us free choice, but He also has 'Plan A' for each one of us, even though, I believe, He still loves us unconditionally if we choose His 'Plan B'. Augustine said, 'O Lord, grant that I may do thy will as if it were mine; so that thou mayest do my will as if it were thine.'

CHAPTER 4

THE HARD
GREY STONE

As I continued to pray around the subject of singleness over
several months, God gave me an impression of a hard, grey
stone with words around the edge of it. I couldn't read all of
the words but as I studied one, God led me to the next. They
summed up how I sometimes felt as a single person at that
time – desolate, oppressed, deserted, rejected, alone, hard
and worthless.

Alongside the stone was a picture of a precious jewel just
like the one my friend had seen, but without the mud around
it. I could identify with the words around the grey stone
so easily, and yet I was conscious that I should be able to
embrace the positive ones around the jewel (see Chapter 5).
So began my life-changing journey through the Scriptures,
using the words around the pictures as a basis for my study.

Desolate

Desolate means comfortless, dreary, lonely or being laid
waste. How many of us feel like that at times? Our enemy,
Satan, loves to paralyse us with such feelings, so preventing
us from being effective in God's kingdom. Much potential
is laid waste when we persist in dwelling on negatives about
our marital state.

In Ezekiel 36 we read of the land of Israel being desolate,
deserted and unfruitful. The enemy had sought possession of
the land so God's people had been 'ravaged and hounded …
from every side' (v.3). They had become the object of people's
'malicious talk and slander' (v.3); only 'desolate ruins' (v.4)
had remained. However, we read in verse 35: 'They will say,
"This land that was laid waste has become like the garden
of Eden; the cities that were lying in ruins, desolate and
destroyed, are now fortified and inhabited."'

Likewise, God's heart is for desolate places, minds and hearts to become fruitful today. The battle for us is often in our minds. We listen to the enemy's malicious talk and slander as he seeks to intimidate us. He whispers destructive remarks in our ear:

> 'I wonder why you're not married.'
> 'There must be something very wrong with you if you're not married.'
> 'Maybe God has forgotten you.'
> 'It must be your appearance.'
> 'It is your personality.'
> 'You're not marriage material.'

I have had many unhelpful comments from other people, too:

> 'What a waste that you're not married!'
> 'You must be a career girl, then, if you're not married.'
> 'Haven't you met Mr Right yet?'
> 'Pray for a husband. I am sure God will give you one.'

When you are feeling vulnerable, such remarks are not conducive to the feel-good factor! Satan is the father of lies and he loves to sow his weeds into our desolate minds. How easily we let them take root and grow so that we become lonely, depressed and comfortless. If only we were more familiar with God's seeds of truth, His promises, His words of life! If we are not rooted in those, any good seeds people seek to sow into us will get blown away, because good seeds do not grow in undernourished soil – many weeds grow there.

Thankfully, the wasteland of Israel in Ezekiel's vision became like the Garden of Eden, the place where, before the Fall, humanity enjoyed uninterrupted fellowship with God.

Jesus longs to draw near to comfort us, but we pull away, our minds full of self-pity – and we wallow in it! Some of us do not want to accept being single, even for a short time, in case God thinks we are settled and decides not to introduce us to our future spouse. As if God thinks like that! How foolish we are, how easily deceived! We will be better wives and husbands if we have learnt to resist the enemy's accusations and lies, and learned to appreciate Jesus' desire to gather us to Himself for protection. Jesus said, 'O Jerusalem, Jerusalem, you who kill the prophets and stone those sent to you, how often I have longed to gather your children together, as a hen gathers her chicks under her wings, but you were not willing. Look, your house is left to you desolate' (Matt. 23:37–38).

The idol

Single people can easily find themselves in a desolate state. Some tend to make an idol out of the marriage issue so that their entire energy is focused on it. All perspective gets lost and 24-hour vigils are held, day in, day out, just worrying about whether marriage is around the corner, how the right person can be met and so on. It is indeed a waste; a waste of time and strength. Worry doesn't rid tomorrow of its challenges, but it robs today of its happiness. When one makes a mountain out of a molehill, one often has to climb it.

It is very different if a person feels called by God to set aside time to pray about a future partner. This is a positive approach; life can be enjoyed and can be productive rather than being 'on hold'.

Let us see the issues at stake and stand firm in our faith as we seek God. We need to be wise and let God, rather than the enemy, renew our minds.

Count your blessings

Around the time I was particularly considering the subject of singleness, I happened to be walking along a street when my attention was drawn to a lady of about my age, who was in a wheelchair. Her face radiated peace and joy. I had been bemoaning my lot as a single person wanting to be married but with no one in sight. I suddenly felt challenged by God to think about my perception of my life. I always thought of my half-empty glass and things I didn't have, rather than my half-full glass and all the blessings I actually did have. I thought about that lady who couldn't walk, run, move about freely or do half the things I could do and yet, here she was, radiating love to everyone and making a difference in the street that day. I had probably reflected misery and self-pity! One life can have a huge effect on others.

I felt lovingly chastened by the Lord. I went home and cried, repenting of my attitude of ingratitude and vowing not to let self-pity overtake me. But I reminded God that I still would like to be married!

A trip to a developing or war-torn country can have the effect of putting everything into perspective and making us grateful for all we have. Creating a list of all the good things we so easily take for granted can likewise be a humbling experience.

Stretch, enlarge, lengthen and strengthen

The passage, referred to earlier, which has helped me countless times over the years is Isaiah 54:1–3.

> "'Sing, O barren woman, you who never bore a child;
> burst into song, shout for joy … because more are
> the children of the desolate woman than of her who
> has a husband," says the LORD. "Enlarge the place of

your tent, stretch your tent curtains wide, do not hold back; lengthen your cords, strengthen your stakes. For you will spread out to the right and to the left; your descendants will dispossess nations and settle in their desolate cities.'"

Verse 3 commands us to enlarge, stretch, lengthen, strengthen, and not to hold back.

It is easier for us to exist in a passive mode, waiting for our imaginary husband or wife to arrive by helicopter on our personal landing strip, but life is a God-given gift to be lived, lived to the full, reaching out to others to bless them, extending God's kingdom.

John Wesley once said, 'Do all the good you can, by all the means you can, in all the ways you can, in all the places you can, at all the times you can, to all the people you can, as long as ever you can.' I may be one but I can influence many for good.

Ruth, in the Bible, was rewarded for reaching out and caring for Naomi, even leaving her land to go to a foreign place. She rose above her feelings, enlarged, stretched, lengthened her relationships and did not hold back. She was rewarded with a kinsman-redeemer in Boaz, and was included in the lineage of Jesus.

Whether or not we get married, we are similarly called to reach out to others. As single people, we are often more readily available to go places and do things than married people. God-given opportunities often have a limited shelf life, so don't miss them! William Carey said, 'Expect great things from God, attempt great things for God.'

As we move on in Isaiah, we read God's words to Israel: 'For your Maker is your husband – the LORD Almighty is his name – the Holy One of Israel is your Redeemer; he is called the God of all the earth' (Isa. 54:5). As a Church, we are collectively a bride. What a blessing!

Oppressed

To oppress means to lie heavy upon, to treat with injustice, to load with heavy burdens, to crush, to smother or to overwhelm. Many people on their own for whatever reason, have claimed to feel oppressed by the way in which they are treated – even by paying single supplements at hotels! Yet God has such compassion for the oppressed. Let us look at some relevant verses, often referring to widows:

> [The LORD] upholds the cause of the oppressed ... The LORD watches over the alien and sustains the fatherless and the widow ... (Psa. 146:7,9)

> A father to the fatherless, a defender of widows, is God in his holy dwelling. (Psa. 68:5)

> Do not oppress the widow or the fatherless, the alien or the poor. In your hearts do not think evil of each other. (Zech. 7:10)

> People will oppress each other – man against man, neighbour against neighbour. (Isa. 3:5)

> 'Because of the oppression of the weak and the groaning of the needy, I will now arise,' says the LORD. 'I will protect them from those who malign them.' (Psa. 12:5)

> Religion that God our Father accepts as pure and faultless is this: to look after orphans and widows in

their distress and to keep oneself from being polluted by the world. (James 1:27)

Defend the cause of the weak and fatherless; maintain the rights of the poor and oppressed. (Psa. 82:3)

He [Jesus] was oppressed and afflicted ... By oppression and judgment he was taken away. (Isa. 53:7–8a)

God works on behalf of the oppressed because He loves them and sees their suffering. He has even experienced it Himself.

Deserted

Deserted means left, forsaken or abandoned. Several years ago I was in India, being taken around various towns by an Indian Christian. One day, whilst my friend went to buy two train tickets, I was left to wait on the only free square foot of the overcrowded platform. I waited and I waited and I waited.

I had no idea where we were going, nor which train to take. Not being able to read Hindi, I really didn't know where I had come from either, as I had only arrived a day or two before, in the middle of the night! I was jostled and pushed from every direction and found it difficult to remain glued to my spot.

Had I been forgotten? What should I do if my friend did not turn up again, or could not battle through the heaving masses? I began to feel more than a little disturbed. I felt abandoned, forsaken, not knowing what to do or where to go. As single people, we can easily feel like this. Thankfully, I eventually saw the recognisable figure and I was rescued. God can rescue us too, if we *want* to be rescued. Feelings of desertion are not in God's heart for us.

God makes no mistakes

Whilst we know that God makes no mistakes, we do
sometimes wonder if He has forgotten us while we wait for
Mr/Miss Right to come along. I felt ready for marriage by my
late twenties and thirties, but suddenly the thought came to
me that my future husband may still be on God's anvil, being
prepared for me. I comforted myself with that thought for a
while. (I have since decided that, if after several decades of
hammering, he's not ready, he's probably not worth having!)

Fulfilment, not desertion

In Isaiah 62:4–5,12 Isaiah speaks of the Jews who had been
deserted and left desolate in their captivity in Babylon. The
promises also apply to the Christian Church of today, of
which each born-again believer – married or single – is a
part. Instead of these two words of reproach – deserted and
desolate – we read, 'No longer will they call you Deserted, or
name your land Desolate. But you will be called Hephzibah
['my delight is in her'], and your land Beulah ['married'];
for the LORD will take delight in you, and your land will be
married' (v.4). Verse 12 says that we will be 'called the Holy
People, the Redeemed of the LORD; and … called Sought
After, the City No Longer Deserted'.

Whilst this applies to us collectively as God's people, it
also applies individually. Desolation and desertion are not
a part of God's plan for any of us. We need to hold firmly
to the truth that God takes delight in us. Let us also set our
hearts to delight in Him.

Rejected

Rejected means put aside as unsatisfactory, excluded,
discarded or renounced. Divorced people particularly

experience these emotions. Jesus understood what it meant to be rejected, even if in different circumstances. He was despised, rejected, oppressed, afflicted and suffered many things for us. But *He* died to set *us* free from rejection.

> As you come to him, the living Stone – rejected by men but chosen by God and precious to him – you also, like living stones, are being built into a spiritual house to be a holy priesthood, offering spiritual sacrifices acceptable to God through Jesus Christ. (1 Pet. 2:4–5)

Single or married, we are chosen to be a part of God's spiritual house. Yes, chosen, not rejected!

Signs of rejection
Rejection can cause us to withdraw to avoid further pain. We can close up and never allow ourselves to bless others with the love of Christ. We see the world through distorted spectacles, and can easily become isolated, miserable and depressed. 'Nobody loves me, everybody hates me!' we cry. We so readily take offence and often keep people at a distance. Rejected people can easily reject others before they get rejected themselves. They would rather not get involved in relationships than risk being hurt.

Other people cope with rejection by chasing round in a frenzy of constant activity to dull the mind and to avoid facing past and present pain. The only way I know to cope with pain is to go through it. We need to ask a trusted friend to pray with us as we face the issues head on.

Big shoots, deep roots
Rejection often has deep roots and affects so much of our lives. If you are a gardener, you might know what it is like to

be forever pulling up weeds from crazy paving. The paving slabs are so tightly packed together that you can't get to the roots but somehow those beastly weeds keep on forcing themselves upwards. The only way is to lift the stones and thoroughly dig out the roots. The roots deep inside us often condition our behaviour. People see the shoots, but we know about the roots – or do we? Sometimes situations that caused our issues with rejection occurred when we were very young, but God can reveal these to us so that they can be prayed through.

'Celebrate Recovery'
In some churches, people are being helped by a Twelve Step programme called 'Celebrate Recovery', begun in Saddleback Church in California.[1]

The course gives people time to look at hurts, habits and hang-ups of the past in a safe, supportive environment. Rejection is one of the commonest problems people have to face, but there is a way out of it in God; so, draw near to Him and be free to enjoy healthy relationships.

Alone

I once read an amusing newspaper article in which the author wrote that he had been excluded from a dinner engagement because he was on his own. He bemoaned the fact that the dinner organisers only wanted couples, just like Noah's ark! We live in a society where single people have been in the minority but, due to increased family breakdown, people on their own are no longer rare breeds!

Some more gregarious singles choose to share homes together to avoid being alone. Sadly, suspicion surrounds single households nowadays, whereas a few years ago it was perfectly acceptable to live with friends of the same sex. As Christians, God knows our hearts and our motives so let us continue to live in single households where it is appropriate. Mary, Martha and Lazarus lived very happily together as natural brother and sisters. Our homes can be special places of rest and refreshment for other single and married people, as theirs was for Jesus.

Completeness

If you are physically alone in life, you are often seen as incomplete. Yet if you look at the way in which God has created our bodies, some organs like the lungs, ears, eyes and kidneys work best in pairs, but other organs, such as the mouth, nose, heart and stomach, are created to work alone. I believe that God equips us to work in the way best for us. Some people are better yoked to another person, whilst others function better alone or in a wider team.

Having said all this, it is still challenging when we have to enter a room of people on our own, and even harder going to weddings, funerals and other church events where there are often lots of very happily married people. I asked Jesus to fill the areas of my life where I did feel half-complete. My testimony is that He did just that; I don't know how He did it, but I know that He did. After all, He had had first-hand experience!

Jesus' example

What a blessing that we have Jesus' life as an example to follow! Jesus effectively said that He was not alone; He stood with the Father (see John 10:30). Jesus never saw Himself as being alone and we need not think we are either, because our Father, who knows us intimately (as we read in Psalm 139), is always with us. Tom Wright quotes a Scottish poem by an unknown author in one of his excellent commentaries.

> I'd rather see a sermon than hear one, any day;
> I'd rather one would walk with me than merely
> show the way.
> The eye's a better pupil, more willing than the ear;
> Fine counsel is confusing, but example's always clear.[2]

'One Solitary Life'

I was once given a card entitled 'One Solitary Life', also by an unknown author, with the following description of Jesus.

> He was born in an obscure village, the child of a peasant woman. He grew up in another village where he worked in a carpenter's shop until he was thirty. Then for three years he was an itinerant preacher. He never wrote a book. He never held an office. He never travelled two hundred miles from the place where he was born. He did none of the things one usually associates with greatness. He was only thirty-three when the tide of public opinion turned against him. He was turned over to his enemies and went through the mockery of a trial. He was nailed to a cross between two thieves. When he was dead, he was laid in a borrowed grave. But nothing could keep him in that grave. Three days later he arose!
>
> Nineteen centuries have come and gone and today he is the central figure of the human race and the leader of mankind's progress. All the armies that ever marched, all the navies that ever sailed, all the kings that ever reigned have not affected the life of man as much as that One Solitary Life.

Jesus' life may have appeared a solitary life, but He lived in community with His Father and the Holy Spirit. The pain for us as single people arises when we feel lonely. Remember, however, one can also be lonely in a marriage, and in a crowd. Whilst being single, Jesus was rarely alone but travelled about with the twelve friends He had gathered around Him. He frequently stayed in a single household with Mary, Martha and Lazarus.

Seeking the presence of God

Over the years, I have made a conscious effort to remember that Jesus is always with me wherever I go. Brother Lawrence, who continually sought the presence of God, says:

> The time of business does not differ from the time of prayer; in the noise and clatter of my kitchen while several persons at the same time are calling for different things, I possess God in as great tranquillity as if I were on my knees.[3]

We too can prove God's promise to be with us all the time as true; even though we may not *feel* Him near, we will just know it. In daily life, I make an effort to talk with Jesus about decisions to be made, work to be done, the use of time, leisure, money and countless other things. I talk to Him throughout the day about anything and everything.

I have found that going for a walk and praising God for some of the amazing aspects of His creation focuses my attention on Him rather than on myself; it brings perspective to realise just what miraculous things God has done. Sometimes I listen to Christian music, pray, sing or read my Bible as well as studying biographies of great Christians of the past and present. I have tried to learn passages of

Scripture over the years, and have done Bible studies based
on a word or subject. I have prayed through the promises of
God and claimed them for myself and others. In these and in
many other ways we can 'practise' the presence of the Lord
just as Brother Lawrence did many years ago.

Be proactive
One Bank Holiday, years ago, before I had read Brother
Lawrence's *The Practice of the Presence of God*, I was sitting
in my flat when the enemy starting plaguing me with his
lies. I suddenly felt very lonely and listened carefully to his
accusations, watering the seeds of untruth in my mind.

> 'Everybody is out enjoying themselves and you're left
> on your own.'
> 'Nobody cares about you.'
> 'I wonder why you're left out.'

I recognised the signs of the gaping black hole that I could
easily slip down. I knew I needed to take action, so I grabbed
my coat and went out for a walk. Unfortunately, a church
family came along, stopped and said, 'Hello, how are you?'
'Oh, fine, thank you! I'm just out for a walk,' I replied. That
made everything ten times worse and my tears began to flow
as they hurried away. It was easily the loneliest Bank Holiday
I had ever spent. After that, I decided to be more proactive
and organise something for the next holiday. Yet I knew that
just filling the time was not the answer; I needed to learn to
fellowship with the One who knew what being physically
alone felt like, and who would understand.

We should preserve those special times with God as Jesus
did when He withdrew from the crowd. To be content on
our own is a great gift; we no longer have to fill every minute

with activity and wear ourselves out. We can begin with
short times on our own and ask God to help us in being
alone physically, but not lonely.

Some singles are natural loners and have to work at being in
company. We are created to live in community. 'God sets the
lonely in families ...' (Psa. 68:6) because He knows our need
of accountability, support, love, acceptance and friendship. I
have tried (but not always succeeded) to live a balanced life of
being with people, but also treasuring times alone.

Hard

Another word around the grey stone was 'hard'. A hard
heart is incapable of feeling love. Frozen emotions and hurt
can cause us to become hard, insensitive and unfeeling.
Emotions such as disappointment, rejection, fear, frustration
or worry can become compacted as we push them down
within ourselves. Our outer protective wall is impenetrable.
We curl up like an armadillo to protect ourselves. We can
turn away from God and become hardened; Paul writes in
Hebrews 3:15: 'Today, if you hear his voice, do not harden
your hearts ...' However, we don't need to resort to that
protective stance.

In Ezekiel 36:26, we read: 'I will give you a new heart and
put a new spirit in you; I will remove from you your heart of
stone and give you a heart of flesh.' Jesus' heart never became
hard as He interacted with people. His Father's love flowed
freely through Him daily.

Frozen emotions
Some trusted friends once challenged me about my frozen
emotions and suggested they prayed for me. I wasn't sure
that I was prepared for this! But after some time, I realised

that one of my strategies for coping with singleness in the
early days was to shut down my emotions. I knew that I
needed prayer, so I consented. I repented and yes, the tears
flowed, but I felt released and able to be myself again. I
vowed to share my emotions more readily so that I did not
need a de-compacting session too often!

Worthless

At my most vulnerable stage, in my twenties and thirties,
sometimes when I saw a child run into the arms of its parent,
or a husband holding hands with his wife, I had a sense of
being worthless. Nobody was that dependent on me or needed
me. I felt valueless, worthless and not accountable to anyone.

Every life has value

A Christian friend, with whom I once shared a home,
suffered from severe depression. She was a very likeable
girl with a promising career ahead of her. However, she felt
that her life was worthless. Regularly, she claimed to hear
voices in her head feeding her lies about herself. However
much encouragement she was given, it seemed to have little
effect. Nevertheless, she eventually emerged from the spell
of severe depression and returned to complete her course
at university.

Sadly, some months later she took her own life. She was
worth so much to God, to her family and to those who knew
her, yet in her eyes her life was of no value. Whilst we know
that she, as a Christian, is with the Lord, there are many who
lose their lives in such a way without knowing God.

Years later, I shared the story at a meeting and a lady came
up to me afterwards and said that she had planned to take
her own life that evening but, after hearing about my friend,

she had recognised the enemy's tactics and was choosing life rather than death. We have a powerful enemy who should not be underestimated, but greater is He who is in us than He who is in the world (1 John 4:4).

Helpful guidelines

Here is a list of helpful guidelines to remind us of our true identity if we have a low self-esteem and feel worthless. We must try:

- Not to speak negatively to ourselves or about ourselves. We can recognise and acknowledge our weaknesses, but seek to overcome them rather than forever dwelling on them. God strengthens us in our weakness.
- To recognise our God-given strengths, and learn to encourage ourselves appropriately.
- Not to be tempted to imitate or compare ourselves to anyone else. We are all unique, not carbon copies!
- To acknowledge that God lives within us, focusing on our potential rather than our limitations.
- Not to be oversensitive to people's comments and/or criticism. Let them develop us instead of discourage us.
- To remember that not one of us is perfect – we are still a work in progress!
- To focus daily on our greatest source of identity, confidence and hope – the God who lives in us!

No life is worthless; each is a gift, each has great value before God.

Having considered the negative words around the hard grey stone, I realised God wanted to change my wrong perception of singleness, to renew my thinking to be more in line with His heart for me as a single person.

CHAPTER 5

THE PRECIOUS JEWEL

What contrasting words I saw around the precious stone! Yet I could not identify with them at the time; they did not reflect how I saw myself. I set aside time to study and pray over each – chosen, valuable, Bride of Christ, wholehearted, diadem.

Chosen

In our games lessons at my secondary school, the teacher often chose two captains who selected their teams from the crowd of us who were standing around in fear and dread that we would not be called until the bitter end. If you were a friend of either of them, you were in with a chance of an early picking, and if you were an outstanding games player you were also a popular choice.

However, if friendship or ability didn't win you an early place on either side, you just made up the numbers at the end. If you came into that category, you felt ghastly and just wanted to hide indoors hugging a warm radiator while everyone else sped around the pitch.

Thankfully, in the kingdom of God, things are very different. God doesn't choose us according to our ability, personality or marital status. The following verses show how God calls us:

'But you, O Israel, my servant, Jacob, whom I have chosen, you descendants of Abraham, my friend, I took you from the ends of the earth, from its farthest corners I called you. I said, "You are my servant"; I have chosen you and have not rejected you. So do not fear, for I am with you; do not be dismayed, for I am your God.' (Isa. 41:8–10)

'But now, this is what the LORD says – he who created you, O Jacob, he who formed you, O Israel: "Fear not, for I have redeemed you; I have summoned you by name; you are mine."' (Isa. 43:1)

'Since you are precious and honoured in my sight, and because I love you, I will give men in exchange for you, and people in exchange for your life. Do not be afraid, for I am with you …' (Isa. 43:4–5)

'You did not choose me, but I chose you and appointed you to go and bear fruit – fruit that will last.' (John 15:16)

'If the world hates you, keep in mind that it hated me first. If you belonged to the world, it would love you as its own. As it is, you do not belong to the world, but I have chosen you out of the world.' (John 15:18–19)

God chooses us to be a part of His family out of a heart of unconditional love. He sees the potential in us, and He is prepared to work on us and with us. What love, what grace! We will never be discarded as useless or rejected as unsatisfactory. However, whilst God chooses us, we don't always choose to obey Him. He has given us free will and our choices have consequences. God has often spoken to me and others through a question: 'Are you willing to …?' God gave me a choice regarding marriage and I made my choice freely.

Jonah bore the consequences of an unwise choice, as did many characters in the Bible. Through fear of not getting married, sadly, some single people have made an unwise choice and the consequences have been dire. Better to be happily single than miserably married!

Second-choice worlds

Viv Thomas has written an excellent book entitled *Second Choice: Embracing Life as It Is*. Very few people live in their first-choice world with everything working out as they had planned it. The majority of us, at least in part, live in a second-choice world. Viv says: 'Second choice situations can become places of grace, community, imagination and maturity.'[1] The book describes the life of Daniel, a man who lived victoriously in his second choice world of Babylon after he had been taken into exile. Centuries later, we still read of his example. We believe that Daniel was also a single man.

In our Western culture today, we expect to select our jobs, homes, spouses, hobbies, and to have free choice in most decisions we make. Not many single people have chosen to be in that state, particularly people who are widowed, separated or divorced. It is probably our second-choice world, even though we are God's first-choice children. How we respond to our second-choice world determines who and what we will become. We either respond to our situation by embracing it, or we react negatively to it – we have a choice. Negative reactions to painful things in our lives sour our attitudes and can make us bitter. In Ephesians 4:31, Paul urges us to be ruthless with bitterness and get rid of it. Our response to situations is our responsibility, even though the situations we may find ourselves in may not be of our making. True fulfilment comes to those who have devoted themselves to something greater than their own well-being.

Valuable

Some years ago, a family friend died and left me her engagement ring. It didn't look particularly special, but I treasured it as a memory of her. One day, I decided to have it valued and was completely overwhelmed by how much it was worth.

Do we see our lives as valuable? Our heavenly Jeweller says of us that we are so valuable that He has engraved us on the palm of His hands and He knows how many hairs are on our heads. We are made in His image; like diamonds, every one of us is unique. Diamond cutters take pebble-like stones from the ground and skilfully transform them into dazzling jewels that have the ability to reflect light. The only perfect, flawless diamond is Jesus, but we are works in progress, the aim being that we can reflect His light and love to the hurting world around us.

Saved for a purpose

The value God placed on my life was impressed upon me when I was twenty-six, the year I had planned to be married! I was driving along when suddenly a car coming in the opposite direction, driven by an old man who had fallen asleep at the wheel, careered across the road and pushed mine up a pavement and through a wall. I eventually heard my rescuer shout, 'She's alive!' Miraculously, I climbed out unscathed from my car, which was a write-off. I stood shaking on the pavement when I heard almost an audible voice saying, 'You are saved for a purpose.' I knew it was God speaking to me. From that day, I knew my life had value. Every life has value.

For many of us, our value comes from what we do rather than from who we are. God does not entirely agree with that perception! However hard we work, we cannot increase the love God has for us. He has no favourites, though He treats us differently. We are of value because of who we are, made in His image.

Bride of Christ

I referred in Chapter 2 to the description of the Bride of Christ; in Revelation 21:2, we read: 'I saw the Holy City, the new Jerusalem, coming down out of heaven from God, prepared as a bride beautifully dressed for her husband.' The bride of Christ, the new Jerusalem, the Church are all names for God's people. In Isaiah 62:5 it says, 'as a bridegroom rejoices over his bride, so will your God rejoice over you.'

The Bride of Christ has certain hallmarks:

- She is very beautiful
- She is beautifully dressed
- She is holy
- She is protected
- She is full of praise and prayer
- She is of infinite value
- She is full of joy.

What a contrast this picture is to the one we have of ourselves individually and as a Church! Yet, as we totally submit our lives to the Father, He will prepare us to meet our heavenly Bridegroom.

Our heavenly Bridegroom

As Christians, married or single, we are betrothed to Jesus and we are in the waiting period, preparing to love, honour and know our Bridegroom. Jesus has gone ahead to prepare a place for us and is interceding for us.

The ten virgins in Matthew 25 found that choices have consequences, with only five of them prepared for the coming marriage. The bridegroom was a long time in coming – some of us can identify with that! It is how we prepare ourselves in the waiting period that counts. Five of the virgins had no oil in their lamps, but the wise virgins were ready with lamps ablaze. Are we ready? We have a choice as to how we live leading up to the greatest of all wedding days. Such choices can have eternal consequences. Let us keep our lamps alight with the fire of the Holy Spirit, renew our minds by reading God's Word, and be joyful and love one another. We are to reflect Jesus, His name, His nature and His glory to those around us.

Wholehearted

Paul writes in 1 Corinthians 7:32–35: 'I would like you to be free from concern. An unmarried man is concerned about the Lord's affairs – how he can please the Lord. But a married man is concerned about the affairs of this world – how he can please his wife – and his interests are divided. An unmarried woman or virgin is concerned about the Lord's affairs: Her aim is to be devoted to the Lord in both body and spirit. But a married woman is concerned about the affairs of this world – how she can please her husband. I am saying this for your own good, not to restrict you, but that you may live in a right way in undivided devotion to the Lord.'

Spend time with the Master
Eugene Peterson translates the passage in *The Message*, 'All I want is for you to be able to develop a way of life in which you can spend plenty of time together with the Master without a lot of distractions' (v.35).

Wholeheartedness, single-mindedness and devotion to God are often looked down upon in our modern world, with pictures of nuns and monks locked up in convents and monasteries coming to mind. Keeping busy with packed diaries is seen as success, rather than time spent with the Master. Living in wholehearted devotion to the Lord has always been my desire, and it still is to this day.

Healthy hearts

A healthy physical heart is created to take in and give out; the extent to which we get this in balance will largely determine our wellbeing. A human heart has auricles and ventricles to take blood to and from the heart. Whilst they are working in tandem, all is well. It is the same in our spiritual lives. Sadly, some of us want to be 'given to' all the time, not only by God, but by other people. We can be very demanding and end up by wearing other people out.

In contrast, others of us give out and give out until we are spent. A whole heart takes in and gives out. We must do the same. It is beneficial to have a Holy Spirit pacemaker fitted to our spiritual heart. He will show us when it is time to draw aside for time with the Master, and when it is time to be a channel of God's love and blessing to people around us.

Throughout Scripture we read of married and single people who lived in wholehearted devotion to the Lord and were chosen for special tasks. Jeremiah was given a word from God about the restoration of Israel; he said the leader would be one who would devote himself to God (see Jer. 30:21). Hezekiah was known as someone who lived in wholehearted devotion to the Lord (2 Kings 20:3; Isa. 38:3; 2 Chron. 31:21). Caleb followed God wholeheartedly and, as a result, entered the promised land (Num. 14:24).

It is easy to develop hardened arteries and veins through having an unhealthy lifestyle so that the blood cannot pass through. Likewise, we can have hardened spiritual blood vessels if we do not guard our minds and spirits. I believe it has been stated in medical journals that there is not a tissue or organ in our bodies that is not influenced by the attitude of our mind and spirit.

Diadem

A diadem is a crown, a jewelled headband signifying royalty. In Exodus 39:30 we read of Aaron and his sons, as priests in the Temple, putting on their priestly robes. These included a 'plate, the sacred diadem' which was made of pure gold and engraved with an inscription such as found on a seal – 'Holy to the LORD'. This was attached to the turban then placed on the priest's head. What a place to put it! If only our minds were holy to the Lord, what anguish we would save ourselves!

A renewed mind

Paul reminds us in Romans 12:2 'Do not conform any longer to the pattern of this world, but be transformed by the renewing of your mind. Then you will be able to test and approve what God's will is – his good, pleasing and perfect will.'

When we study the Scriptures, we will get a more balanced view of celibacy alongside marriage. George Müller, founder of many children's homes, said that he considered it a lost day if he had not had a good time over the Word of God. William Booth, founder of the Salvation Army, said that the greatness of a man's power was in the measure of his surrender. All this begins in our minds and spirits.

Let us set aside time daily to read God's Word so that we may indeed test and approve God's will for our lives. As single people we can be extremely busy, coping with all the tasks normally shared between two in a marriage, but let us seek to spend quality time in the Word. I feel sorry for young married people with small children who are woken at the crack of dawn by little voices, and from then on never have a minute to themselves until bedtime. Let's make the most of our quiet room to speak with our Father daily.

Paul exhorts the Corinthian church not to be 'deceived by the serpent's cunning' or their minds will be 'led astray from ... [their] sincere and pure devotion to Christ' (2 Cor. 11:3). Paul tells the church that he is jealous for them, as he has promised them as a pure virgin to one husband, Christ Himself (2 Cor. 11:2).

We are all, single or married, precious in God's sight, chosen, valuable, part of the Bride of Christ, called to be wholehearted and holy in our thinking and in the way we live. Let us accept these truths and live in the light of them.

CHAPTER 6

THE PASSIONATE SEARCH

Whilst some people enjoy being single and, indeed, have chosen to be, other people may not relish the prospect; instead, they may be thinking to themselves, 'I am desperate, determined and passionate about getting married. My pillow is soaked each night with tears of sheer anguish as I see my friends and siblings finding marriage partners. I feel incomplete, lonely, upset with God and at a loss as to what to do.'

Passive or active

Paul in 1 Corinthians 7:8–9 says, 'Now to the unmarried and the widows I say: It is good for them to stay unmarried, as I am. But if they cannot control themselves, they should marry, for it is better to marry than to burn with passion.'

Perhaps some people are too passive in their quest for a marriage partner, hoping that the ideal person will just appear as they sit at home and wait. Others take matters into their own hands and leave a trail of disaster behind them. Our passions can, at times, lead us to make foolish choices. We look longingly at every person of the opposite sex we meet and ask, 'Is this him/her?'

In 1 Samuel 16:7 we read of the dangers of being drawn by outward appearance alone, and in Proverbs 31:30 we are reminded that 'charm is deceptive, and beauty is fleeting'. Imagine your potential partner in ten, twenty, fifty years time and ask yourself if you think you will still be attracted to him or her.

How, when, where?

So how, when and where do we find the right person? How should we, as Christians, pursue our desire for marriage?

- Pray. When Jesus was desperate, He submitted His will to His Father (Luke 22:42).
- Find a trustworthy person or people with whom you can share your feelings, and who can pray alongside you.
- Write down some non-negotiable points – for example, 2 Corinthians 6:14, which states that believers should not be unequally yoked with unbelievers. (There have been rare exceptions to this when a spouse is converted after matrimony, but these cases are not the norm.)
- Write some desirable qualities you would wish to see in your spouse.
- Live your life!

Where we meet people will vary according to our lifestyle, but whilst a 'sit at home and pray' approach may be right for some, it may be unfruitful for others. Talking to married couples, I find that they have met in countless different ways:

- At work.
- At church.
- At school, college, university.
- On singles holidays.
- At church camps, conferences, seminars, etc.
- By joining interest groups or evening classes, eg sports, music, crafts, walking etc.
- By internet dating – the January 2007 edition of the magazine *Christianity* contains an article on internet dating. The author of the article, Catherine Larner, suggests that whilst dating agencies used to be frowned upon, now opinions are changing. Nevertheless, she rightly sounds a note of caution and advises singles that personal recommendation is preferable when selecting a website. Not all agencies have a strong faith ethos, even

when they claim to be Christian.
- At national and local singles groups.

The way in which people meet their partner is perhaps less important than the absolute assurance that the person they have met is the right person to marry. (It is also worth adding here that whilst some may have found their spouse through the internet, others have only found heartache and disappointment.)

Praying and waiting for God's best is one of the hardest things God asks us to do, but it is worth it. Being sure of God's guidance can be challenging when desperation has set in, but it is possible for those who really, sincerely seek it. Psalm 32:8 states: 'I will instruct you and teach you in the way you should go; I will counsel you and watch over you.'

God's guidance

Many good Christian books have been written on the subject of guidance which must spring out of a relationship with God. Usually a number of factors come together like a jigsaw:

- Verses of Scripture
- The witness of the Holy Spirit
- The witness of trusted family and/or friends
- Circumstantial signs
- Our God-given intelligence.

The peace of God in our hearts is one of the most reliable ways of knowing God's will, even if it does mean waiting. Clearly, emotions come into play when we are searching for marriage partners, so this will be another vital sign – but not the only one to rely upon.

John's testimony

One of the hardest choices I've had to make as a Christian was to remain single as long as I have. I had met a friend of a friend and really liked her, but wasn't sure what she thought of me. Have you ever had that kind of nervous feeling? If you have, it was probably something like that.

She was only around occasionally, but when I saw her again I liked her even more, and sensed there might be a connection. We talked about various things, including where we thought we were going next with our lives, and then she mentioned that she was called to Brazil.

It was as if there was a record that slowed down and stopped, or as if a curtain came down around us. I was called to stay in the UK, this was already clear. So I couldn't ask her out. To be honest, I started choking up a bit and actually wanted time to speed up so I could go off and cry somewhere.

After I left, I was angry with God. Why had He done this? I had finally met someone, only to have our separate callings get in the way. I talked it all out with Him, hot tears and all, until I was calmer. I knew I would have to let go, and it was like a knife in my chest to start with, but as He and I spent time together, peace sneaked up from behind and put gentle arms around me.

A short while later, her friends and I were at a social, and they were sounding me out, I think. They asked me what I thought of her. I was totally honest and to the point: 'I think she's gorgeous (and here I paused before going on) but she's called to Brazil and I'm called to stay here.'

They were taken aback, and asked if I was sure. Shockingly, I was. The conversation moved on to other things, and that was the end of that. I knew I'd done the right thing, but that fact didn't make it any easier. There are certain things that God and I settled a long time ago, and for destiny to kick in, they need to be adhered to no matter what. But that was a real test of my commitment.

I'm still single for now, and still looking for a green light. I know that there are single women around, and I hope to find someone my own age to go out with. I know that God plans to bring someone my way, so I wait for His leading as I meet new people.

I refuse to *settle* for someone just because they are available. I want the best match, the sort of woman God has in mind. For now, I exercise as much faith and discernment as I can, and ask God for more when I lack them. And every so often, I go through the pain barrier and move on; temporary troubles, life as usual.

Simon's testimony

I became a Christian when I was a child. When I reached the age of eighteen, I had a whole range of ideas, fears and expectations about the future. Would I meet the right girl someday? Was I homosexual? Would I ever have children? At a Christian camp, God radically changed my perspective. I felt Him say to me, 'Are you willing to do anything for Me?' I was willing, and had a real love for the Lord, but I was not prepared for Him saying to me: 'Would you be single for Me?' He led me to Matthew 19:10–12. In tears, on the floor of a marquee I remember sobbing, 'Your will be done, *Lord*!'

I had really been asking the wrong questions. The right one was to settle who was Lord of my life! Over the next couple of years, I settled the issue that I could genuinely remain single for Him, and live a satisfied and abundant life. Seven years later, at the age of twenty-five, I was even asked to speak at a 'Satisfied and Single' seminar! It was only once this issue was really deeply settled that God miraculously revealed the next step of His plan.

As a single man, I had to overcome the frustration of family and friends 'matchmaking' for me! This was intensely painful as I knew that, while they had my best interests at heart, most did not seem to take on board the possibility that I may remain single. On the other hand, as a single man without a girlfriend or other relational ties I was free to enjoy university without added baggage, feel free to travel abroad, and was especially able to pursue the most important relationship, my relationship with my eternal Father, Brother, Master, Friend, Counsellor and Lord. In this there was peace.

Simon is now happily married with two delightful children, having met his wife at a party. He wrestled with the rightness of the relationship, having settled the issue of staying single. However, God made it clear that he should pursue the friendship, and it ended in marriage.

Other people may find themselves still single but increasingly fulfilled. Knowing that God is in sovereign control of our lives is the only real key to peace and joy. Seeing ourselves in partnership with God, working in His kingdom, can take away – or at least reduce – the feeling of desperation.

CHAPTER 7

SINGLES IN OUR CHURCHES

How do we, as the Church, see ourselves as single people? Do we see ourselves as a hard stone or as a precious jewel? Not only can our perception of God and of ourselves determine our effectiveness in His kingdom, but the view of the Church on our marital status can also affect us. It is so important to foster understanding, respect and support between married and single people in our fellowships.

How can we welcome and pastor single people in our churches today? Singleness needs to be talked about as the God-given best for some people *alongside* marriage, rather than it being sidelined for the few 'odd' ones, the ones who missed God's 'Plan A'.

There is huge potential lying dormant in some of our churches where singles are not valued and used for their gifting; in other churches, the assumption is that singles have endless time on their hands to serve in countless ways, regardless of their talents. They are often dismissed because they cannot measure up to the norm set wrongly by the Church that everyone should be married. There may be a lack of grace, understanding or support for those struggling with the issue of singleness, whether this is a result of being unmarried, separated, divorced or widowed.

Mandy's testimony

From a very young age, one of my heart's desires was to get married and have a large family. After a couple of relationships, at the age of seventeen I met a lovely Christian student at my church, Richard. We soon felt that God was in our relationship, and four years later, after I had spent a year in India and started my nurse training, we got married. Over the following few years we were blessed with four wonderful children.

Life was great with children, good friends, church, love and laughter. Richard was a wonderful, loving, caring husband, father and friend. I remember saying one day to a good friend that I found it hard sometimes to have a deep relationship with God because Richard fulfilled all my needs. Sadly this was not to continue.

One day when we were on holiday in Scotland with wider family, Richard went out for a bike ride alone. When he didn't return, we discovered that a car had driven into the back of him, and after a few hours he died in hospital. After thirteen years of happy marriage, I was left a widow at the age of thirty-four, with four young children aged twelve down to six to bring up alone. I remember one of my early thoughts was, 'But I never wanted to be a single mum!'

Overnight, life changed beyond belief. Having been in a serious relationship from the age of seventeen, I had never really experienced being single. I was now, suddenly and unexpectedly, totally alone. At times I felt very vulnerable. I no longer had my soulmate to share day-to-day life with, to chat over the concerns about the children, or just to be with and have fun. Bringing up children with two parents is incredibly hard work, but on your own could easily become overwhelming! My parents were so good, but they lived 400 miles away. I was very blessed to have a friend who moved back in with us temporarily (and stayed four years), but she could never have the same personal care and interest as a husband and dad.

Other people in the church didn't know how to cope with Richard's death, or how to treat me. Although Richard and I had been leaders in the church for many

years, I found I was very rapidly dropped. I am sure
that the other leaders probably felt they were helping
me by not laying anything extra on my plate, but it
would have been so nice if they had discussed it with
me! I felt like I had become obsolete – no longer a
valued member of the team.

One of the things that I found hardest, particularly
after moving to a new area, was the fact that I no longer
seemed to fit in anywhere. I didn't seem to be included
in couples events because I wasn't part of a couple,
but I didn't feel single people accepted me into their
circles either because I had children with their related
responsibilities. In retrospect, I should have invited
people over to visit me more often, but the truth of it
was that it was hard enough keeping my head above
water with caring for the children and the house to
consider what my needs were.

Despite what seemed an incredibly sad situation in
which to find myself, I was amazed at God's incredible
grace. I have never felt as close to God and cared for
by Him. The poem 'Footprints' has always been very
precious to me, but during those early bleak days I
can truly say I know God carried me. I came to know
Him in a way that I never had before. Romans 8:35–39
says that nothing can separate us from God, and that
was certainly my experience. Another of my favourite
passages from the Bible is Psalm 139, and in verse 16
it says that even before we are born God knows how
many days we will live – this made it comparatively
easy for me to accept the death of someone in the
prime of his life. Knowing that Richard had gone to
be with his Lord and Saviour, and was now in a better
place, helped me tremendously. I met together every

week for the first year with a very precious friend who prayed with me. I chose to dig deep into God and He came close to me. Having said all that, there were still some days that I really wished that God had 'skin on'; times when I just wanted to have someone to give me a hug or snuggle up in bed with.

Over the next few years, I tried to always look for the positive in situations. One 'silver lining' to this cloud was to meet and become good friends with the recipient of one of Richard's donated lungs. It was very precious to see the gift of life that came from his death. Another was that I was able to move and enrol my children in the Christian school that we had always wanted them to attend. I know that certain of the teachers prayed for and encouraged them on many, many occasions. A few men in particular were very key in being good Christian male role models for them, and made a real difference in their lives.

After six years of the usual ups and downs of life, God blessed me with a lovely new husband and five wonderful stepchildren. This again has kept us constantly on our knees as everybody gradually adjusts to what our new family is. Nine teenagers can certainly cause headaches, but can also be lots of fun. Some years on, we are still a work in progress. Having had some tough times, most of the relationships are now good. What I can say is that God has been with us all throughout. Although I would rather not have had to walk the road, I am also grateful for all that God has shown me through this time, and the relationship I now have with Him. None of us know what the future holds, but I do know that if we reach out to the Lord, He knows the way and will gently lead us.

Mike's testimony

How is it that God could put His seed into the line of
David, with its history of sin, debauchery, murder,
adultery, prostitution and more? Yet at a time of
grieving I feel judged by my own conscience. I expected
(perhaps wrongly) disapproval from my local church.

This is the fundamental issue that I and many others
face as we seek reconciliation with our conscience and
with others who misunderstand us as we cope with
relationship breakdown. It's true to say that we are
not looking for excuses; we readily blame ourselves
for our own failures. As men, not to be able to 'fix'
a relationship almost falls into the same category
as not being able to mend a leaking tap, or provide
financially for our family. Even with our knowledge
of God and His grace, we are more ready to condemn
than forgive ourselves.

There is no doubt that God walks with me, and He
shows me daily that He loves me, and provides for me
in ways which seem both remarkable and exceptional,
often breaking my own preconceptions of what I think
would be 'acceptable' to God; yet some parts of the
Body of Christ find such difficulty in coming to terms
with failures in life. We (and I include myself) believe
as Christians that God longs to bring forgiveness –
but how do we deal with relationship breakdown as a
church when one of our own fails what seems like the
ultimate test: to stay married?

The friendship circles and bonds of trust we knew
as a married couple often disintegrate when our new
status is single, until such time as we have created a
new identity. The choice to move church and reappear
in a new life seems all too tempting and is apparently

the commonest way of dealing with the bereavement that comes from seeing all our friends and church relationships fail just because we are no longer part of a couple. But to stay in the same church presents its challenges; to live with other people's struggles in relating to our new status and yet to find God's peace and heart often seem so difficult.

We talk of opening the church to the world around us where relationship breakdown is a familiar and everyday experience, but how can we welcome such hurting people when we so often don't understand the bereavement and pain that occurs in one of our own? To go to a weekly meeting, or share a dinner once a month or a house group once a week might be helpful, but when one is trapped at home night after night, wanting to find love and acceptance, one can feel very alone.

God is, however, remarkable; let us keep our eyes on Him and He will walk with us through the pain and into reconciliation with ourselves and others. This will not happen immediately; it takes a long time to find God's grace and peace again after all the feelings of rejection and isolation.

For me, I am grateful to those who have stood by me with understanding, and to my church leaders who have walked the painful journey with me. I believe the Church is stronger as it learns to love without condemnation and accept salvation and redemption for all, regardless of their circumstances. There is no hierarchy of sin and, in fact, as we are *all* sinners, we are *all* looking for a place of forgiveness through the salvation of a loving God who wishes to draw us into eternity in full relationship with Him. This I long for as I take another step through another day with my own failures – but in God's grace. I know His touch and accept His life within, and thank Him that He is truly a Father, having chosen and adopted me as His son and lavished on me every spiritual blessing day by day. For this is Christ's love for a hungry and thirsty land, lost without hope, grieving for what it doesn't know it has lost and longing for what it hasn't yet found.

These testimonies reveal the pain felt when, for whatever reason, marriages end; and yet, both individuals refer to the amazing grace of God in such situations. In churches, the subject of broken relationships surely needs to be addressed. People are looking for a safe place to recover, and for help in readjusting to being one again instead of a couple.

Various churches have organised events and groups for people on their own. However, some singles loathe being labelled as a 'single' and are not inclined to go to singles' groups, whilst others welcome the fellowship of like-minded people who understand them. Single parents often long for helpful guidance on bringing up children on their own. We won't please all the singles all the time because we are all so, so different. Each church needs to hear what would be best for the singles in their fellowship.

Many single people prefer to be included in God's wider family. Married people with young children are busy, but could be so blessed by singles who may enjoy being spiritual aunts, uncles and grandparents. It is also true to say that many singles would welcome help and support with challenging practical tasks! Time is at a premium for singles working full-time, especially for those who are trying to cover the work of two parents. The continual transporting of children to school and other activities, tending the garden, sorting out the problems with the car, cleaning the house, shopping, washing and ironing seem endless at times. Discussing our single and married states will foster understanding, respect and support for one another. The perceived idealism of both states can be addressed and realities faced, as well as some practical help being made available.

Thoughts from Eleanor

Church culture appears to be primarily set up around families and couples. Certainly in a lot of churches, singles are definitely not represented on leadership teams. This may imply an unconscious thought that singles are not worth as much as a married couple. Perhaps we need to be more proactive in creating opportunities for leadership for those single people who clearly have leadership potential.

There are not as many men in the Church as there are women. How, then, can women achieve the 'norm' of being married? Where do we reside within a church body?

When we look at society at large, there is an increasing reluctance to get married early – or at all – and this, too, is bound to be reflected within the Church (within the culture in which we live). But how do we, as Church, react to this changing world?

Sexual temptation

We live in a world where we are surrounded by sexual temptation. Is the Church addressing this issue through effective teaching and support for individuals? Having a gift of singleness doesn't mean that sexual temptation is removed or that people are especially self-controlled. The media would have us believe that we cannot survive without sex but, contrary to modern opinion, sex is not vital to life! Sex is not an uncontrollable instinct. Sex is a God-given gift – but as Christian single people, called to be celibate, we can control our appetites. It depends where we focus our attention. Corrie ten Boom prayed, 'Lord Jesus, You know that I belong to You one hundred per cent. My sex life is yours also ... I believe You can take away all my frustrations and feelings of unhappiness. I surrender anew my whole life to You.' [1] She testifies that God answered her prayer.

In his excellent book, *I Kissed Dating Goodbye*, Joshua Harris encourages singles to ask themselves these questions:

- Am I concentrating on 'simply pleasing the Master?'
- Am I using this season of my life to become a 'holy' instrument for God?
- Or am I scrambling to find a romantic relationship with someone by dating?
- Am I failing to believe that God is sovereign over this part of my life and can provide for me?
- Could I possibly be throwing away the gift of singleness?
- Am I cluttering my life with needless complications and worries of dating? [2]

Jesus said, 'Blessed are the pure in heart, for they will see God' (Matt. 5:8). Purity – amongst other things, keeping sex for marriage – is not a popular concept in our modern world, but it is God's way, and is the best way. Intimacy and commitment go together, not intimacy and short-term relationships.

In 2 Timothy 2:22 we read: 'Flee the evil desires of youth, and pursue righteousness, faith, love and peace, along with those who call on the Lord out of a pure heart.' Many single people who have chosen to walk God's way have admitted that the lust of the eye is a real temptation. In 2 Samuel 11:2, we read of David walking around on the roof of the palace when '… he *saw* a woman bathing. The woman was very beautiful…' (my italics). Unfortunately for David he did not turn away, so he got deeper and deeper into the mire.

Both married and single men and women have testified that personal boundaries need to be set, such as deliberately averting the eyes when beautiful girls or handsome men pass by, not watching certain late-night television programmes, or refusing to go to pornographic websites. Sadly, however, some people have become addicted to pornography to fulfil their sexual desires. It is a battle, and it may take time, but healing and restoration are possible. Bringing temptations into the light by sharing them with someone else often robs them of their power. Being accountable to someone else is also a helpful way of 'walking clean' in this area of sexual temptation.

Daniel's testimony

Scripture contains neither a commandment nor a recommendation to be married. The expectation in some churches is often that those who are single should not engage with the opposite sex except to pursue a meaningful, longer-term relationship which has the expected potential of leading to marriage – for what would be the point of companionship, friendship, mutual benefit otherwise? For many people, however, meaningful friendships exist with the opposite sex without complication or undertones. Clearly, wisdom needs to prevail in the setting of boundaries – for example, it is not wise to give a friend of the opposite sex a lift home late at night when we are feeling tired or vulnerable.

But what of desire, and lust, even sex? It has always puzzled me that we assume that before marriage, young and older people can somehow separate themselves from their sexuality, waiting only for the moment of union in marriage to consummate their desire. Did they suddenly change at the point of marriage to somehow become something they were not before? Of course not – they were always sexually aware. But what if there is no suitable partner to marry? We forget that for many young people (and older!) the chemistry of our bodies and the lust of our eyes can fill us with a consuming desire which cannot be immediately satisfied. This is not to say that anything is permissible just because it burns within us. However, to assume that outside marriage we simply do not know such desire is nonsense and denies the nature of our creation.

Some struggle with desire, passion, even lust, knowing that it is a battle of the good within and the evil that torments. Unfortunately, the scenario for many people is even more complex than this, and is potentially more difficult for those who have been married, or perhaps have had more than one partner during their lifetime.

For those that are married, it seems to be easy to set the gold standard, assuming that in marriage sex is a unique blessing, providing love and comfort and commitment, sharing each others' bodies as Christ loved the Church. To the single person, it is a torment that in a modern world, filled with such profuse images of sexuality, they should struggle to meet the expectations of their married peers; some even become confused about their own identity and values. Without understanding, single people are likely to suffer in silence. What can make this worse is the way in which sexual sin is often ranked higher than other sins, leading sometimes to the chastisement of offenders, sometimes publicly, often by those who are in secure married relationships.

It seems that as we allow our worship of God to transform our lives, we enable God's power to work within us and change our desires. I have never, however, met a single person (young or older) for whom this transformation has been an instant salvation. It is clearly incumbent on the whole Body of Christ to seek to support, encourage, teach and admonish one another that we might run the race to which we have set ourselves. In all circumstances, we know that no temptation has overcome us that is not common to humanity, but we know also that God is faithful and will not let us be tempted beyond our strength, and that He will provide a way of escape (see 1 Cor. 10:13).

When we become Christians we are adopted as God's children; there is no doubt that our Father loves us. When we fail in His expectations and the Spirit within us convicts us of sin, we recall that He sent His Son to pay the penalty for our sin. Desire has the ability to fulfil marriage, but also to destroy the Christian through temptation and sin, particularly in secret. In my opinion, we should not permit the enemy to win this battle. If all other sins are forgivable then let sexual sins also lead to repentance and not condemnation. The gospel is a restorative gospel, and our hope and help for each other should be the same. Let us sharpen and encourage each other to maintain a life that is worthy

of our calling, but stand with those who fall, raising all
to the hope that is within them.

'How Christian single adults can change the world'

Clayton Coates, former singles' pastor at Saddleback Church,
California, says this:

> When God decided to establish his Church and restore
> his relationship with us, he sent his Son, Jesus Christ.
> Now he could have said, 'You know, I desire for my Son
> to be married. When he is married, more people will
> listen to him, repent and believe.' ... He could have
> done that but he didn't. ... His desire was that his Son
> remained single while seeking and saving the lost and
> leading others to repent and believe.[3]

Clayton goes on to say in his article that churches have
focused on married adults to meet all the needs of the local
church. Consequently, most leadership positions have been
held by married people so that singles receive the message
that they are not up to it. The important point is made
in Clayton's article that in God's kingdom we are made
complete in Christ rather than through marriage to a partner.
Three questions are put to pastors:

- How can you motivate single people to play a significant
  part in the local church and be leaders within it?
- What should your encouragement be to singles in the
  church?
- In what ways could you stand alongside three single men

who are zealous for God, who could enhance
your ministry?

Louise's testimony

I think undoubtedly there are many opportunities for
service that singles can take up that are perhaps not so
readily available for families. It may be easier for the
single person to be released from their situations so
that they can venture into something quite new, even a
move to another nation.

Families often face far more complex issues, especially
when considering an overseas move – the financial
budget can multiply quickly, and children's ongoing
educational needs can be very challenging and costly.

What may limit singles in pursuing new and exciting
ventures may not be the lack of opportunities – I feel
sure they can be found – but the courage to take a
leap into the unknown by oneself. (How much nicer
it would be to have someone come with us!) My
experience is that it is scary, but also very exciting,
when one is confident it is the Lord who is opening a
new door. I moved to Hong Kong in early 2003 and it
is still surprising to me how much I feel at home in a
foreign culture, and with a language I do not speak.
I am fulfilled (and stretched) in a work that I believe
in and feel called to. I dreamed but never imagined I
would see so many interesting places and experience
such diverse cultures. I am so glad I took that step
to follow what was in my heart, however difficult it
seemed at the time. It was so worth it. There have been
some very tough situations and experiences too – but
that's life! The support of friends and family back home

make it all the more possible – and cheap international phone calls and internet services provide easy and accessible communication.

It is, without a doubt, hard at times to be single. I find this especially if I am travelling in faraway places on my own – but how exciting the opportunities are! And I have found that God is always faithful – He is always with me.

Issues of singleness and loneliness do not disappear when we move into a new situation or a new location, and I know for me these will continue to surface from time to time, and each time I have to deal with them and call upon the Lord. But it helps tremendously to know I am in the right place, and in His purposes. Though I have come to appreciate time on my own, it is so important for me to connect with other people. I don't believe we were made to live in isolation, and the Lord is faithful in providing friendships. These are vital and are a precious gift from the Lord.

Hannah's testimony

The one thing I missed, being single, was having a family of my own. Although I was teaching children there was still emptiness inside. God has been very gracious to me over the years and, sixteen years ago, I met up with a family at Spring Harvest. We became good friends and have been very supportive of each other over the years. I spend Christmas with them and I was blessed when one of the daughters said, 'Hannah must come for Christmas; she is one of the family.'

A vision for our lives

I long for the Church to see more of the possibilities
for extended families. Everyone ends up somewhere! A
clear vision, along with the courage to follow it through,
dramatically increases our chances of coming to the end
of our lives feeling that we have made a difference. We all,
married or single, want to feel that our life counted. Vision
gives meaning to otherwise meaningless tasks. Taking
the detail of daily life in the context of a God-ordained
vision gives meaning and purpose. Vision is vital for every
individual and every church; as we read in the King James
Version, Proverbs 29:18, we will 'perish' without vision.
How wonderful it would be if churches had a vision to
recognise and use everyone's gifts and talents regardless of
their marital status. Whether they do or not, my message to
single people is to rise up, fix your eyes on Jesus and pray for
doors of opportunity to open up that give scope to use your
God-given personality and gifts to bring glory to God and
to bless others.

Rise up, single man, single woman; fix your eyes firmly
on Jesus; see the potential in yourself as one person to make
a difference, even to one other person's life; recognise the
plans God has for you at this time, and live a Spirit-filled life
to bring glory to God, blessing to others, and to be fulfilled
yourself. It is only in Jesus that we can be *truly* fulfilled.

CHAPTER 8

HELPFUL SUGGESTIONS FOR SINGLES

These are some tips which may help us to overcome some of the challenges we face as singles as we seek to live our lives for God, furthering His kingdom alongside families.

1. Hold a *plumb line* against your thinking, attitudes and behaviour from time to time. Ask yourself if they are true to plumb with the Word of God, or whether you are swayed by the current thinking in society, or even in the Church. We read of God speaking to Amos about judging His people because they were not true to His plumb (Amos 7:7–9).

    This will provide protection from Satan's lies which flood our minds and distract us from the work God has for us to do. Immerse yourself in God's Word so that you know His promises and can 'keep straight' in your thinking.

2. Keep a pair of *'spiritual binoculars'* to hand. Look ahead to see what is happening in the lives of your peer group. Then be prepared! Ask God to give you grace to cope with the events of their lives, and to be able to truly rejoice with them. Be ready for their:

    *   marriages
    *   birth of children
    *   children's dedications, christenings, etc
    *   children's graduation and other successes
    *   children's marriages
    *   birth of grandchildren
    *   silver, ruby, golden and even diamond weddings.

    One of the secrets to overcoming the tendency to become bitter or vulnerable to temptation is to be aware of our weak areas. Satan knows them and wants to trip us up, so let us heed Peter's advice to stay alert, resist him and stand firm in our faith (1 Pet. 5:8–9).

3. Keep a check on the *balance* of your life. Try to keep a balance of the following:

- time spent with people and time spent alone
- time spent with families and with singles
- work and leisure
- giving and receiving
- serving and being served
- learning to be content and making the most of opportunities.

Ruth's testimony

'Are you prepared to be single for Me?'

This was the question I felt the Lord ask me as I stood with my back to a tall hedge in the garden of an English country house. I was a student, and I was on a 'weekend' with other Christian Union students. But this was a very private moment between the Lord and me. The question was unexpected, and yet I felt the Lord wanted an answer.

I looked into my heart. Part of it had always wanted to be married and have children. Yet there was also a very real desire, a deeper desire, to be single-heartedly devoted to Jesus. I hesitated, unsure how to respond to such a question. But then, as I looked at the Lord, the answer became clear to me and I yielded my life afresh to Him with *all* my heart. I answered, 'Yes,' and immediately a beautiful, light-filled peace from God flooded my being.

Since then I've been working out the consequences of that decision!

- It's been about accepting and trusting God's good plan for me, when I would have chosen a different path for my life, and over time realising that God *is* good to me and being *glad* that He's planned my life the way He has.
- It's about realising that I don't have to have children of my own to be a mother in the kingdom of God, and that
- I don't have to have a house of my own to have a home.
- It's about strengthening oneself in God *before* facing family gatherings when everyone else has a partner, or *before* taking a walk in spring when every person and every creature seem to be in pairs!
- It's about having a positive strategy when returning to an empty flat after experiencing constant friendship, fellowship and fun over a holiday or conference.
- It's about giving no room to self-pity, speaking sternly to one's soul with words such as, 'Eyes off self and eyes on God'.
- It's about being thankful for the things I *can* do as a single woman.
- It's about realising lots of romantic novels, films and music are unhelpful. The damaging effect of the media, which so often seems to promote sex, can be overcome by not having a television!
- It's about cultivating relationships with close friends, and letting them be physical arms around me when I know I just need a hug.

- It's about keeping holy relationships in view when working alongside men – married or single.
- But most of all it's about pressing into God and getting to know Jesus as my Best Friend and the Husband who will never ever leave me. It's about sharing any concerns for the future with Him, and about hearing Jesus reassuringly promise, 'I will be faithful to you.'
- It's about cultivating a love language of songs and scriptures with the Lord, and about sharing these regularly with Him.
- It's about remembering that I can never 'outgive' God!

> I have a friend whose faithful love
> Is more than all the world to me,
> 'Tis higher than the heights above
> And deeper than the boundless sea,
> So old, so new, so strong, so true;
> Before the earth received its frame,
> He loved me – blessed be his name!
>
> (*I Have a Friend* by C.A. Tydeman)

The best way we can prepare ourselves for marriage or for singleness is to love the Lord our God with all our heart, soul, strength and mind, and to love our neighbour as ourselves (Luke 10:27). God's ways are higher than our ways, His thoughts higher than our thoughts (Isa. 55:9). Trust Him!

We have the gift of one life on this earth. Let us view our lives not as insignificant, incomplete, incapable of making a difference, but full of boundless opportunity in the One who is Father, Son and Holy Spirit, and who says, 'Never will I leave you; never will I forsake you' (Heb. 13:5).

NOTES

Chapter 1

1   Clayton Coates, article written 21 February 2007 for Rick Warren's ministry, Tool Box. Used with permission.
2   Camerin Courtney, www.christianitytoday.com/singles/newsletter/mind40811.html (11 April 2004).
3   Corrie ten Boom with Jamie Buckingham, *Tramp for the Lord* (London: Hodder and Stoughton, 1974), p.156.
4   Joshua Harris, *I Kissed Dating Goodbye* (Sisters, Oregon: Multnomah Publishing, 1997), p.44.
5   Sir Cliff Richard with Penny Junor, *My Life, My Way* (London: Headline Book Publishing, 2008), pp.194–195.

Chapter 4

1   See www.celebraterecovery.com.
2   Tom Wright, *Paul for Everyone: Galatians and Thessalonians* (London: SPCK, 2002), p.100.
3   Brother Lawrence, *The Practice of the Presence of God* (London: Samuel Bagster & Sons Limited). Undated in author's copy.

Chapter 5

1   Viv Thomas, *Second Choice: Embracing Life as It Is* (Milton Keynes: Paternoster Press, 2000).

Chapter 7

1   Corrie ten Boom with Jamie Buckingham, *Tramp for the Lord* (London: Hodder and Stoughton, 1974), p.157.
2   Joshua Harris, *I Kissed Dating Goodbye* (Sisters, Oregon: Multnomah Publishing, 1997), p.80.
3   Clayton Coates, article written 21 February 2007 for Rick Warren's ministry, Tool Box. Used with permission.

RESOURCES

- Al Hsu, *The Single Issue* (Leicester: IVP, 1997).
- Heather Wraight, *Single – The Jesus Model* (Leicester: Crossway, 1995).
- Helena Wilkinson, *Beyond Singleness* (London: Marshall Pickering, 1995).
- Steve Chilcraft, *One of Us* (Milton Keynes: Word, 1993).

WEBSITES

Before beginning to look for a potential partner on the internet, make sure you are using a valid Christian dating site. Even so, exercise much caution; remember, people are not always who they seem in cyberspace!

www.christiansinglestoday.com
www.christianconnection.co.uk
www.christianevents.co.uk
www.eventsforchristians.co.uk
www.friends1st.co.uk
www.londonchristians.co.uk
www.networkchristians.com

National Distributors

UK: (and countries not listed below)
CWR, Waverley Abbey House, Waverley Lane, Farnham, Surrey GU9 8EP.
Tel: (01252) 784700 Outside UK (44) 1252 784700

AUSTRALIA: KI Entertainment, Unit 31 317-321 Woodpark Road, Smithfield,
New South Wales 2164. Tel: 02 9604 3600 Fax: 02 9604 3699

CANADA: David C Cook Distribution Canada, PO Box 98, 55 Woodslee Avenue,
Paris, Ontario N3L 3E5. Tel: 1800 263 2664

GHANA: Challenge Enterprises of Ghana, PO Box 5723, Accra.
Tel: (021) 222437/223249 Fax: (021) 226227

HONG KONG: Cross Communications Ltd, 1/F, 562A Nathan Road, Kowloon.
Tel: 2780 1188 Fax: 2770 6229

INDIA: Crystal Communications, 10-3-18/4/1, East Marredpalli, Secunderabad
– 500026, Andhra Pradesh. Tel/Fax: (040) 27737145

KENYA: Keswick Books and Gifts Ltd, PO Box 10242-00400, Nairobi.
Tel: (254) 20 312639/3870125

MALAYSIA: Salvation Book Centre (M) Sdn Bhd, 23 Jalan SS 2/64, 47300 Petaling
Jaya, Selangor. Tel: (03) 78766411/78766797 Fax: (03) 78757066/78756360

Canaanland, No. 25 Jalan PJU 1A/41B, NZX Commercial Centre, Ara Jaya,
47301 Petaling Jaya, Selangor. Tel: (03) 7885 0540/1/2 Fax: (03) 7885 0545

NIGERIA: FBFM, Helen Baugh House, 96 St Finbarr's College Road, Akoka, Lagos.
Tel: (01) 7747429/4700218/825775/827264

PHILIPPINES: OMF Literature Inc, 776 Boni Avenue, Mandaluyong City.
Tel: (02) 531 2183 Fax: (02) 531 1960

SINGAPORE: Alby Commercial Enterprises Pte Ltd, 95 Kallang Avenue #04-00,
AIS Industrial Building, 339420. Tel: (65) 629 27238 Fax: (65) 629 27235

SOUTH AFRICA: Struik Christian Books, 80 MacKenzie Street, PO Box 1144,
Cape Town 8000. Tel: (021) 462 4360 Fax: (021) 461 3612

SRI LANKA: Christombu Publications (Pvt) Ltd, Bartleet House,
65 Braybrooke Place, Colombo 2. Tel: (9411) 2421073/2447665

USA: David C Cook Distribution Canada, PO Box 98, 55 Woodslee Avenue, Paris,
Ontario N3L 3E5, Canada. Tel: 1800 263 2664

For email addresses, visit the CWR website: www.cwr.org.uk

Day and Residential Courses
Counselling Training
Leadership Development
Biblical Study Courses
Regional Seminars
Ministry to Women
Daily Devotionals
Books and Videos
Conference Centre

Trusted all Over the World

CWR HAS GAINED A WORLDWIDE reputation as a centre of excellence for Bible-based training and resources. From our headquarters at Waverley Abbey House, Farnham, England, we have been serving God's people for over 40 years with a vision to help apply God's Word to everyday life and relationships. The daily devotional *Every Day with Jesus* is read by nearly a million readers an issue in more than 150 countries, and our unique courses in biblical studies and pastoral care are respected all over the world. Waverley Abbey House provides a conference centre in a tranquil setting.

For free brochures on our seminars and courses, conference facilities, or a catalogue of CWR resources, please contact us at the following address:
CWR, Waverley Abbey House, Waverley Lane, Farnham, Surrey GU9 8EP, UK

Telephone: +44 (0)1252 784719
Email: mail@cwr.org.uk
Website: www.cwr.org.uk

CWR Applying God's Word
to everyday life and relationships

OVER 100,000 COPIES SOLD IN 7 LANGUAGES

Your
Personal
Encourager

BIBLICAL HELP FOR DEALING
WITH DIFFICULT TIMES

Selwyn Hughes

Strengthen yourself and others with biblical insights
Your Personal Encourager

This revised edition will enable you to encourage yourself and others in times of stress and difficulty.

Drawing on more than four decades of counselling experience, Selwyn Hughes deals with forty of life's most common problems, including fear, disappointment and bereavement.

Topics addressed include 'when God seems far away', 'when hopes are dashed' and 'when doubts assail'.

by Selwyn Hughes
96-page paperback, 130x197mm
ISBN: 978-1-85345-072-3
£4.99